Collage

Peter Lloyd was born in the English Midlands
and emigrated to Australia in the late 1970s.
Most of his working life has been dedicated to
providing housing for the under-privileged. He
lives in the Adelaide Hills and is married with
two children. Peter has had work published in
Australia, Canada, the United States, the
United Kingdom and France.

collage

Peter Lloyd

Wakefield
Press

Wakefield Press
Box 2266
Kent Town
South Australia 5071

First published 2002

Typeset by Gina Inverarity, Wakefield Press
Printed and bound by Hyde Park Press, Adelaide

National Library of Australia
Cataloguing-in-publication entry

Lloyd, Peter, 1930–   .
Collage: poems.

ISBN 1 86254 570 7.

I. Title.

A821.3

To Rosa

Contents

cartoons & characters

Black Water

Glares a sudden savage Samurai-moon
from a midnight puddle,

the trees blow, clouds race overhead,
a rain-squall is coming in.

When the moon vanishes,
everything vanishes:

now,

with

one

blind

finger –

you write a poem in an inch of black street-water . . .

Three Guitars for Lorca

Six strings accompany huge butterflies
on their journey towards the snow-peaks of Andalusia;

lost souls and the wailing of guitars remember Lorca;

darkness splits the mind,
electric fields of massive power and many unperceived silences

glitter at the corner of the eye/or naked victims
jump from a precipice as a blue wolf howls through a broken
    window

at the invisible falling without wings at the feet of death.

Sometimes, a rose, intricately fashioned from the twined guts of
    humans and horses,
drops from the black belly of war

and the music goes home to die;

Remembering Lorca – ice freezes to death –
mountains cannot forget the clouds nor the wind cover its rocks.

Among the vast snow-peaks in a guitar –

a lone skier plunges down …

        *   *   *

... with a sudden savage chord – in a café, up a cobbled street
   with vines,

an old man sits under the immense darkness of his hat

making reality and dream
become the vast silent decay of a cathedral

from whose crypt
the unborn

stare up blindly at a monstrous sun

through the eyes of his flying fingers ...

          *   *   *

The mountains are peaceful tonight:

Chagall's green donkey is asleep,
a long dark ladder is propped against the stars;

very far away, where a tiny gypsy caravan, painted with castles
   and Castile roses,

journeys round a crescent moon,
the stone face of a woman in earrings looks back ...

   somewhere there is a knife ...

we do not know what is happening:

this is the dark night
in the agony of the lost soul

trapped forever
in the black belly of the guitar.

We would gladly die.

Ooompah

Round and round ...
And round and round and round ...

gaslight
catshit
cobbles

three blind soldiers climbing from a bin,
a collision of ghosts in the mist,
trumpetsbassoonssaxestubers and a drum,

Crohn's, Parkinson's, Strokes, Black Lung, Lupus and Rickets –

all the dead who fall from windows in my mind ...

O my people!

Join our Brass Band Procession.

         *   *   *

On the drumbeat – Thwack!
On the drumbeat – hungry images of broken streets.
Old time terminator robo-cops without mercy and weird
    mind-control!

Punch-whack! Judy thump! Punch/Judy/Punch.

Dysmenorrhoea.

Eyeless windows in a slum.

         *   *   *

Pure and simple – like carved heads of anthracite in the sky:

Money beats religion anyday/Are you washed in the blood of
   the Lamb?

             *   *   *

Weightless shrouds/faces of dead miners underground –
also being some wind-instruments old streets fall from –

NELLY Deane with cabbage soup
ToMMy tucker, you are Mi … marching HomE Again, Silver
   THREads

                                      Among The GOld

When we open the window
to breathe

a legless crutch hobbles away.

             *   *   *

The saxophone
that can't read music anymore,

the tuba missing in action –

in a tented velvet sky hung with zodiac signs, winged horns,
a gypsy telling fortunes gazes at a crystal ball:

shadows are grouped round a mummified piano.
There's breathing in lost fields,

bones and green beasts alike go chomping at golden peaches
   of Paradise.

We seek among stars: sleepwalkers among the mysteries
   of war.

           *   *   *

Round and round –

singing children fall from the clouds . . .

Yellow snot gotta lot
Sloppy trot slimy bot

Down yer bot, smelly sot –
Says one two three – YOU'RE OUT!

far under pit-heads,

brass bands crawl shoulder-deep in mud and blood,
   troglodytes calling through distances,
a million passageways in the dark wet rags of the resurrection
   and the hope –

blowing trumpets

We're alive
We're dead

Two Preludes

Pure Debussy – pure Monet ... millions of *glancing*,
blue-green dancing-gold-blue-vermilion air-motes.

Or heat in langour: a small sailboat at anchor, green-purple
   on stillness:

in 'Sails'* – which might also be the 'Cap d'Antibes' or 'Yachts
   off Ètretat'** –
the seascape is silent, the sun shrouded – when, suddenly, with
   fifteen notes
in the piano treble, ending in a trill – a seagull screeches,

a breeze dips the boat ...

all the colours shift and change –

whereas in Monet they are completely still.

           *   *   *

Now sunset-end,
half-light, silhouetted against the Lake, a black cormorant
takes its shadow through an infinity of time –
and a beautifully polished Steinway goes on endlessly grieving ...

   (... daylong, the hourless, sun-drift Lake,
   mirroring aquamarine-gold-French spindrift mirage of itself,
   has been glimmeringeringering, reflecting cleffs and notes,

   depthless and glittering within the music ...)

Now reeds and moon in a moonmist
rise over the keyboard: a corncrake flies through blue shells
   of crying;

subtle leakages of dark grope like ghosts
in shadow-twilight around the lake –

while Debussy's flaccid hands, shore-scum under the fingernails,
drift this way and that over the piano: a wet skull staring

under a mat of dead weed as gray, soundless birds arrive
  – hieroglyphs
from the underworld carrying more sheet-music in their beaks.

* Debussy's Prelude 'Sails' or 'Voile'
** Seascapes by Monet

Kenko's Symphony

In seeking the ineffable –

'To soften the glare,
By letting new wheels move along old ruts'

Kenko's Symphony of a Thousand is performed
    without instruments:

the concert audience reflects on the transitory nature of life –

the musicians,
sit in complete silence

as they begin 'free each day to take the path . . .'

This Contemplation of the Minimal – an artist's impression of
    black/white/movement
without dead spots or static areas,

is the Power and Beauty of the mind
moving through time and space . . .

a silk painting,
the Aurora Borealis,
deep in the forest of nothingness . . .

I am thinking about The Gate of the Palace, the opening scene
of the first scroll in The Life of Sugawara Michizane . . .

in the soundless singing of bluebirds of distance:
in minds surrounding mine, waterfalls glide through infinity . . .

Thus – sublimity accomplishes without having to act:

*'Without having to look out of the window
One can see the way of heaven'*

When Kenko's symphony comes to its conclusion,
at a signal from the conductor, the orchestra quietly makes
   its exit.

During the applause,

I hear
someone
say –
   I could have written that ...

Arsehole!

Salt

Desolation –

> the silence of salt rising through wheat ...

old Jew-mocker, biblical Gomorrah prophet,

grinning sodium ghost by a broken plough,
cock-sucking a lick of moonlight in its fist.

> They all crumble –

Power Stations, tin cans,
> potato peelings, the essential crystals of
  love letters ...

We walk in the vogue of the foreskin
with the glitterlands of sky-vaginas under our fingernails:

but everything comes down,
the wind blows,

– and all that filthy screaming of people, mouths blackened
  in time,
fists crammed with their own droppings, pounding against
  the sky –

out of nothing,
into nothing,

by the rivers of silence.

Turn of the Screw

Earth-trickles
into stone-fall-dark

– among soft-rot and beetle-tick, I wake again,
to find you ghost-walking through my dreams;

starved in black, your sagging breasts,
by graveyard candlelight,

a shadow picking through ancient history,

a rusty shovel tunnelling under dead flowers,
waist-deep in sleep –

while I, my dust and skulls around me, legs putrescent,

wait patiently ...

patiently – for the sound of fingers fumbling at the screws,

soundlessly in dark for the lid to swing ...
open to the stars again –

for the moment –

> *VOILA!* TO RISE! ...
> SINGING LIKE MIST!

cries echoing! Toothless! Mouth open wide –
a tiny two-headed Christ! a polished coffin full of rotting baby clothes.

– smiling, I watch you stumble back, cold as death-sweat,
high heels piercing the clay, breasts, mouth gaping,

black flowers falling from your eyes ...

(... nor all the King's Horses ...)

Distances

20.5.2000

A packet of poison: a scream alone,
the colour of a bruise darkens the hill –

cool shadows of suicide as mind-echoes echo,
doors open, stairs, hospital corridors curve away,
repeat themselves

by opening into more doors, echoes, distances –

remoteness of deadfall,
isosceles stone ferns in black waterfalls
vanish without ripple into polished floors ...

Illusion is all –

ambiguity between figure and ground,
the terrible distance of blank stone faces,
between flat patterns and apparent 3-dimensional recessions

in which the silence of alienation completes itself
like the faint rim of snow round a distant star ...

when footsteps come

– they walk without touching moon-waters.

But colourless.
Wordless.
No one wants to wake.

cloud after cloud ...

Wool

She's knitted him good this year – leggings,
starbursts for his cancer hat: rainbow of jumpers,

embroideries of plants, lookouts from mountains
and something to feel easier when he breathes;

but smaller and smaller he gets,
yellower and yellower.

Now his feet hardly touch the ground.

But she's knitted him good this year: her balls of wool skein
    down the Avenue,
three ply, four ply, round the bushes, the lampposts, over
    the cars,

round the neighbours, in the evening and the morning:
moss stitch, stocking stitch, any stitch

hemming them in – the glimmer stitch and the moon stitch
    that's too fine to follow

over the sun and the Western Star.

But last night, I saw her at her wits' end in the garden,
a fat, lost neighbour
high in a tree like a spider
knitting black blinds for her eyes
so she'd see no more . . .

know no more –

and something for her ears.

No one 'phones

A wet moon
hangs from a hole in space,

severed mains wires trail from a bed-sit ceiling:

you come to it up the stairs —

beside a Shell gas station, a demolition site, broken floorboards,
a row of lavatories kneeling in the mud:

no one calls,
no one phones:

it is where I am going now towards the king's palace
over the stone hills of town,

past the next street —

and the edge of the world keeps rising towards the stars,
    hitch hiker ...

                    *   *   *

Lion skins, horned helmets. Time-travellers down at the
    Job Centre.
Snarling of Fabulous Beasts, cries of Venusian slave-girls And
    grape pickers
with golden baskets on their heads. How beautiful! the
    endless tragedies
of the Magyars, the lament of the Khassiyem drawn out on a
    six-stringed violin.

By the waters of Babylon.
The one with a butterfly asleep on her lips. She smiled.

*   *   *

Half goat, half horseman
he galloped past over the rooftops of Main St.

Bring me an apple from the Hesperides, I called.

But it was too late, too far.

Bones dropped from the tree a killer wind howled through
    his jaws.
The hairless pelt of a Pukt from the moons of Sirius/also among
    my souvenirs.

*   *   *

All night, whispers from the Universe fill a wineglass held to
    the ear –

brain particles discharge themselves into
pool-glitter stars and the curve of time:

by the excavations –

a traveller at the crossroads
consults the Force: beware the Giant Exotherm and
    weird dissonances
of poisonous remorse, she screams from her kiosk –

But ferrous-sulphate clouds billow from the ground.
Dark rumblings accompany him from the nexus of Retreat.

Ghosts soundlessly pass in weird stretch-limos.

... the trouble is
　　　　the streets
　　　　　　　will claim you in the end, my mother said.

Fool
Jester

The old woman seven years dead.

Old Slop-Bread and Wet Mouth waiting by the bin.

Everywhere, blanks slide down the walls, undulate their shadows,
snapping like dogs at passers-by.

The Invisible Man vaults over rooftops,
two wet eyes for spit: the sores of a cripple that smoke and stink
　like candlelight –

more snapshots to carry like Family through the dark ...

　　　　　　*　　　　　　*　　　　　　*

Until, suddenly, at the Job Centre, a mysterious message
　from Beyond –

Love, meet me at the Western Gate!

(this time from China)　　　　　　　　　　　　　*Signed*

She who waits
In the twenty-leaf album
Of Chen Hung-shou ...

Mist was drifting from the blue mountain:
the Stone Boat from the summer palace.

In pale bloom and very faint stitches/green silk.

Behind the curtain/breathing.

Saltdamp

Saltdamp in fog – by a fresh pile of dogshit,

an old bagwoman waves her stick at midnight bins,
corner of a door between two crumbling walls –

a meeowling cat jumps into her arms forever and again:

their four eyes lock,
ruined-grey by misey,

as the old woman rocks her cat,
as the old cat rocks her woman.

But how far through the Alley, stumbling past the next screaming
    world's end
balled-jawed rat-trap, tongue lolled out and strangled –

or the stone dogs find them by howling round a cirle of bones
and the streets tumble over the edge of dark ...

– *when, suddenly, its mouth engulfs her again – another*
    Vietnamese horror!

– by the Old Church, a ghost of architectural ribs licked by
    angels ...

a moon, drenched by rain, flaps mong tombstones like a
    frightened owl.

        *   *   *

The Old Grey Church

The Old Grey Church has closed,

Our Lady of Mercy and the Dirty Bandages has closed ...

of Christ and the Bloody Needle,
of Grippe and Cancers in the Mouth,
of the Father of Filthy Flowers desecrated by cigarette butts on
    the roundabout,
of Greasy Wrappers and the Great West Window overlooking
    the Takeaway,

of the Lost Child's shoe.

The clergy have fled
and there's broken glass in the gutters.

The Progenitor has gone.

Ice cream and Graffiti are splashed on all the Walls.

           *   *   *

But still how may we now?

This is Vallejo's 'great fallings of the Christ of the soul
from some blessed faith blasphemed by destiny: those
    bloody blows

are the crackling of loaves that burn us at the oven door ...'

when twilight, the colour of a bruise, finds no horizon in the
  streets tonight,

only death rays glittering from pig farms and supermarkets
keep the skies clear; stained glass circles the air:

at broken traffic lights, invisible cripples go on dancing,
imagining God.

A Prayer for Billy Martin

Now enter another planet … gluttony of rainbows with a hi!
  goodbye! now to blossom-drift through chimney-tops –

and a prayer for Billy Martin too,

on his mother's arm,
a plunging shambles flailing up the street –

until a sudden stumble-stop!

gaping,
loose mouthful of clouds,
teeth, tongue …

a head-swing upwards and round that swivels back to

AHH! AHH! YAAH!
SHRILL yYiP!

from some dark spittle-splash centre in his brain …

half animal,
half bird

trying to
trying to

Hi! you say, pointing to yourself –
but strange beasts surround you with weird shadows

and his child's face flies rooftop-off, flapping terribly
into an afternoon's fantastic blue-sugarplum-flowering
  happiness –

and he's gone! gone ...

    until
                another
                                misfire

and spicules, his millions of Picasso fragments return to his
    mother's side ...

and away he swim-lurches, surrounded by swirling angel flights
of unimaginable beings and wondrous hopping, talking birds not
    of this world;

at the bottom of the street, a golden bus drives off
    through the sky ...

his mother waves frantically, a moment of flowering trees and
    tuberoses stayed behind ...

                    *   *   *

Streets

On a wet street-map, was trying to find Breakdown St. today:

with my finger, was trying to trace
Ulcer, Stiff Shit and The Last Chance Shopping Parade ...

For another client,
Plague St. that used to be off Spina Bifida and Lumen Christi
    Way, couldn't find
Needlestick St., Skint St., or Kid Suicide St.

And how about Psoriasis, Eczema and Bad Teeth St.?

... about Can't Pay the Rates-Rent-and-Budget-Funeral St.
back of Ferryman-Jester and the last rowboat leaving
    through the dark?

Making endless lists in the rain today,
watching peoples' faces in the drifting mist and wet,

I reckon, in this city, about 100, 000 of us barefoot saints
wandering tarmac

don't live here.

                    *   *   *

A Whiff from the Dumps

The wind right from Spraycanland and Stubbyworld –

brings a whiff from the dumps,
curtains moving

in a shiftworker's dream ...

a gas bubble belched,

through buzzing bones and nostril-wax
and rotting shirts and shit:

a Cyclops' eye –

crows' flight and stare
from the sleeper's tongue.

Dead cars with blood in their hair drive
through town after town.

       *   *   *

Really, it's a business: forklifts of decay – Italian shoes, maggots,
  Japanese sushi:

electrons from the dump stream up,

the futility of solar bread, a final severance of words
can slam you under the heart like a fist – irreversible ...

horizons drift down
velvet and dead flowers,

they all go: blind owls, charred violins, broken traffic lights.

A distance of fabric held together by fading dust.

Anything salvageable!

– pure zeniths of silver eyelids, golden urns.
Early morning, old men's hands go dipping for treasure
   in mist;

then a bird flies up from garbage onto the rotting door of
   a frig.,
streets slip and fall apart into the sadness of broken crockery.

This is the mystery of the dump – through indecipherable
   swirling atoms,
the Spirit Master goes on looking for lost lives in broken
   picture frames:

– a decaying cushion, an old shoe ...
the mute intensity of one world stares dumbly into another.

              *   *   *

Spring. A ten-year-old cherry pit, rooted by the dump gates,
   flowers again for the Emperor.
Foot of a Zen rock, mountains of tyres attend. In the poet
   Ryokan's begging bowl – violets and dandelions, an offering
   to the Buddhas of the Three Worlds.

              *   *   *

From my Winter Diary, this small prettiness –

– two fox cubs tonight, playing and nuzzling nursing home
   waste, become tangled in bandages:
up on their hind legs, no thought for tomorrow – one rolls over
   dragging a torn sheet, the other

dances in stained frippery ... while the vixen watches, leg raised, a
   filthy tampon in her mouth.

The moon shines. The frost glistens. The world goes round.

And it's Disneyland! It's Bambi in Disneyland again!

            *   *   *

The Green Dwarf,
The Headless Man

The Strutting Crow

La Revolution, les Flags over Cheap-as-Chips and Rent-a-Tele –

Alone now, top end of the estate where garbage trucks roar
   and tip:

Landlordland, Stubbyworld – like smoke –
a breaking wave of pubs and churches around the hill:

gulls ride with tractors on stench thicker than their wings –

until a sudden dust-storm, papers, the air vanishes
and the town flaps among broken laths and glass like an
   ageing moth

come home to a labyrinth far from flowers:

under my feet, a feathered crutch hisses blindly at the sun.

Collage

Further along from an Oriental splash of colour on
    the pavement
and a dead cockroach caught in the grease of a Saturday
    night's takeaway,
the courgettes were scattered – whereas the Bami Goreng,

being hidden by a swarm of Wanderer Butterflies, seemed
more of an exquisite tapestry in gold and black:
the probosces of these spectacular insects

curled and uncurled as they sipped juice and drank
    their breakfast;
their wings flexed and slowly flexed again
like marvellously painted Japanese fans.

All around, the deserted streets and factories –
the silent cogs and wheels of the universe were going
about their own business –

and there's me, Sunday morning, peering over a splash of
    Eastern vomit
on the pavement!

A maverick beauty: is that the phrase I was looking for?

Vortex

Paradise Row, Coffin St, Angel Tce,
Mafeking, Sebastopol, Waterloo,
The Bethel Chapel, The Bottle Shop, The Green Man ...

tick-tock in the clock
says you're back –

and you can't stop it!

... everything becomes swirl-whirl (dust blowing,
factory smoke, dandelions, The Wasteland, Yob-Gob
of pavements as if the aliens have landed back in time
with wheels, belts, pulleys,

a real Spielberg dot com. forward-slash,
chaotic/quantum-century/vortex/

radio static/in which people grope through blind black-
thunder-crash-and-lightning, storm of psychobabble up the street –

and everyone holds onto the next screaming grammar,
tongues lolling and pointing towards howling,

mad-dog-polyglot-horror
in the day-night roar of lavatories)

– it is only after *this* you finally take off your hat
and know you're home and there.

Or, miraculously,
the darkness parts:

a beam of sullen backyard light illumines a rusty
    down-pipe tied with wire –
beside which a certain small flower
still grows towards the years:

through a blue door –

three angels welcome you in.

*   *   *

Toxic shock

Toxic shock

plants in pain

sour planet of midnight news!

The sky billows its moon like a sick prince:
– beware, Seeker of Truth –

valleys of rocks. Nothing is real.

(static hissing in the dark, ghost doors swinging,
as fierce conjunction of Mars and stars circle a cosmic wilderness)

Still they follow you – big white plastic footsteps trail like mystic
   signs to the crossroads:

strange temple of twisted masks in the dark. Devil worship place
of green-machines and guttering candles.

O slick Snake of Lies!

In the Sacred Grove.

Shhh the mad dwarf!

The Clocks

Never quite –

like that three-legged dog moseying
from tree to tree down Coffin St. ...

Time Travel isn't easy
dragging a neighbourhood along;

strange moons drown in the Victorian urinals behind the pub –

but tall trees drag them out
crooning little Listerine tunes to themselves.

The way is long.

Constellation after Constellation: the back streets moan,
cheap watches dream while clothes hoists and dopamine
silently shake themselves to dusty death –

and the Horses of Night stare morosely over the traffic lights.

But who are we, Songs of Disaster,
a savage parade, our fingers chopped off and bleeding –
of the Lost Tribes, in hyper-drive, always lost,

the nearest star   time zones, shifts of the infinite away –

and through all the chiming shaky banging rickety bells and
   Old Clocks of the Universe:
but – what holds it up?

And why are we always halfway there?

One Foot . . .

By chance –
at a car-boot sale, I buy these three for luck:

a quill-feather,
a pair of golden apples
and a Venusian love-offering preserved in cochineal:

dwarfs with kind faces pass hand in hand with centaurs.
The hours pass swiftly; it is rare to hear music like this.

Who can better

my quill-feather,
my pair of golden apples
and a Venusian love-offering preserved in cochineal –

I ask the plum-dark angel with the flaming sword who stands by
    the door.

But the way back through an empty planet
and the sewage works is fraught . . .

howling travels on the wind, at every street corner –

Amulets! Where can we buy amulets against the dark!

Ghastly mould-ladies, mutants,
the ratpacks of the world.

Midnight strikes. Its clock-skin glows like a Nazi Shrine,
the giant white legs of landlords stride effortlessly beside the bus,

terraced clouds leave scorchmarks at the terminus,

and a hag-bird wails.

A world in pain – it waits for you on the stairs like a cripple
    in an old coat –

one foot in front of death,
one foot in front of death –

its mouth open.

The Dark Hair Sighs

Of course – the old want to be physical –

in green highlands of light,
new cliff-tops of imagination

where the hieroglyphs of the rain
make good souse all night.

Dance, says the ghost, relax in the valley –
watching trees and orange-blossom drift from their eyes:

bees and honeysuckle waver with black fruit in waterfall-time;

so what's to fear in an old person's breath?

Kiss me, says the old man,
kiss me, says the old woman.

The old want to be touched,
they want to touch and be touched,

to stroke and be stroked –

to lie in someone's arms
and know its

   yes!
            O yes!

Also white blossom-time, skirts blowing,
cloud-ephemerals and beautiful green leaves reaching
  Springtime upwards.

Mornings like this, when the dark hair sighs for love,
  the geranium
flowers fire on ice – a moment sometimes falls and spins
  like a black rose

into the blue heart of the sun ...

an old man stares at a concourse of shadows/
slip through his fingers ...

over the hill/following him.

A Surprise

A surprise – first light, Nghulli, Totem Emu,
suddenly trots past the Laundromat looking for

Changing Woman –
who also vanishes through a brickwall, leaving
clip-clop of hooves,

diamante earrings dangling like spider webs.

And it's on the dot – in world of mist, half-light and megaliths,
city of dark and dreams –

one year, 31,536,600 seconds have passed – and I have woked!
I'm here just as zero! zero! just as …

Look at the sky! I scream –

And it's irretrievable!

… a sudden flash,
a God-skinning-eyeball-explosion at the omphalos,

as a yellow fingernail, slashed and tipped with crimson
stabs through the mist, a cat yeeeowls,

and cardboard boxes float down the Alley
on a tide of light, an old woman drowns, clutching
   her photographs –

and from faraway, faraway over the horizon, softly comes
the drum-drum-drumbeat, skiffle-skiffle-shh-shh!

       (beside a pile of dogshit
       and a broken door)

of my first fantastically and furiously seeded Dandelion
   of Spring!

as the first blooms stare up at the first moments of the
   newborn-sun.

If I were Monet, these would sell for ten million heartbeats
and some yellow money.

If I were van Gogh,
I'd hide them in a barn.

Over the Wasteland

Over the Wasteland which should be a Gorge,
among the factories and tenements which should be trees,

I can see mountains beginning
with water and moss.

Rice paper flutters: gnarled apricot trees
among village snows ...

from where I'm sitting (by broken prams, old mattresses
black ooze from pipes) to the right, is Crouching Tiger Rock –

striped bamboo-grass in the northeast corner
marks the pond garden at Tenryuji.

In the shadow of a broken Cola bottle
and the remains of a cardboard box –

a butterfly flexes its marvellously purple wings:
willow and wild sumac, bushclover and cypress

bloom inside the gate.

Basho says – go to the pine if you wish to know the pine.
Today, in the tearoom at Kohoan across from the junkyard, I am

studying the fall of light in a dry landscape with stone lanterns.

Dust blows with folded sleeves and bows enigmatically,
sun flashes on the passing windscreen of a Datsun

and a 747 bulges dragonlike through the sky:

beautiful they are – those tiny enamelled sparrows

hopping among exquisitely fronded grasses by their
  oil-drum homes.

As a citizen of this quaint borough to whom recently
a love of Japanese gardens and horizontal scrolls

has quite fortuitously and mysteriously occurred --

may I thank heaven's blessing that happily now accompany
  my every step?

The Offering

Winter, we left with cold winds kicking the place down like
   a hooligan –

weeks later, returning,
were charmed to find the garden door transformed
into a beautifully embellished Fusuma screen painted
with ancient flowering trees and a blue lake, beside which,
pheasants on a gold-leaf background,
were flaunting their tails in fine array.

A purple butterfly was sunning itself beside the path.

That afternoon, drinking tea
in the shade

of our new Stratco carport hung with geraniums –

seemed a fitting place to make an offering after a safe journey
to the Buddhas of the Three Worlds.

And my wife.

Ballast

For ballast, weigh the black,
the sombre and the gray: these colours

are much heavier than clouds.

And to anchor an evening in the sky between two stars —

drop the moon over the mountains
into the mist so that its planetary string or tie

becomes entangled in the swaying branches
of a white apple-blossom tree ...

   (this small Chinese painting, executed in the Time of Spring,

I dedicate now to a thumbnail of cool rice wine

and a small back-garden veranda
I built for myself
last year...

but without thinking about the second moon in the pond.)

Blue Leaves

Excuse me, if, in that journey between Osaka and the sun rising,
I kept touching your breasts,

your legs which were also flying –
though merely with my eyes, was quietly deliberate – say more like
    an ox and cart
being driven by a travelling artist, a pencil,

a peasant, maybe 30, 000 feet down between Jakarta and Istanbul,
gazing up at the sky as the Jumbo passed –

a brush with chinese hair dipped in black/white,

but very delicately and beautifully,

with face, teeth, hands perfectly

filling in mists, valleys, the stillness under a moon
as the first birds began to call –

While you slept and the 'plane flew on under falling blue leaves

in the pale shadow of a silver birch.

Butterflies

It has to be the Fauve's final deathsweat in my mind,
  a palette

of light-Matisse-blue, flecked, green-pink organdie sea-silk
restlessness of wing-bur with late evening and enamelled
  billions
turning dark blue-mist like swirling butterflies,

for depth upon depth, opalescent distances for a
  million miles –

while 30,000 feet below, Japan is going up in celestial
  woodsmoke

and the plane drones on,
touched on a darkening wing

by the first faint blue fingernail of an Oriental moon.

Island Dance

Like *frangos* in the Goat Dance –

and there they went, my clothes,
in shell-fish heaven,

swept from a beach in Skyros ...

or Nureyev and Fonteyn,
shirt sleeves billowing,
a trouser sur-les-pointes,

circling each other
among the dolphins
in green-green depths:

a graceful entrechat here,
a slow arabesque there –

whereas my Nikes, following the sun,
and months later, are probably even now
wading ashore like two unshaven bums

somewhere in Patitiri or Kythnos

(that Kourtaki Red with feta in olive oil:
– one flash of a moment like this –

like drinking in a filthy shirt ... with sunset
going down, a bloodsoaked bib over Italy.)

Or those rats in the crapper at night back of the taverna
where tourists unzip –

in concrete footprints,

and for twenty minutes flower hopelessly as bougainvillea

off one meatball.

Wow!

A sunset riff by Jimmy Hendrix –

transits of Golden Buddhas and body-piercing Wow!

Beads – Flower Children of Siva,
Dharma Warriors swarming through the Milky Way,

and Poetry – a spoonful of warm sperm for the world

  (Ginsberg, Kerouac in mantra-song haven of beatitudes,
  humming Indian love songs with naked feet . . .)

As light fades over rooftops
– out of nothing, into nothing, it flows over you:
the old vanish: only Kali-Darg is real –

Kali-death dancing with wet feet through the spittoons of the
    world . . .
the tambourines are silent:

when skeletal leaves and used toilet paper blow up the
    hallway –
rain spatters on a broken window

and a door bangs in the dark . . .

– in winter, all abandoned squats are the same.

The Indian Wars

Farunder thunder, blue monsoons massing,

the cricket match went on:

there were forty thousand tanks,
half a billion tons of explosives ...

anti personnel mines,
hundred of fighters zoomed,

Christian, Buddhist, Allah ...

Ninety columns of refugees bowled to him,
one hundred and eighty thousand children were killed,

four hundred villages were bombed flat

while he went on batting:

seven hundred thousand were hospitalised,
half a million were widowed.

By the time they brought out drinks,
he'd already

made Cricketer of the War.

Later, with his big toe, he shyly wrote his name –
for the Record Book in the sand – -

which the wind tossed and played with at the Members' End.
And it was Pukka English OK.

Vertigo

... it's like this freeclimb
blind hold –

cliff-face moment of reality,

a sudden crumbling, deadfall slow –
arms legs,

mouth open

clownlike twirl of a rag doll,

becoming smaller and smaller ...

as crags reel,
echo upon echo in an empty sky.

And tiny figures peer down,
frozen in disbelief.

To recur anywhere – the street, the bathroom:

suddenly, the deafening sound of blue clouds,

a lithium mountain looms through the mist –
there's a death-hold of instant sweat,

coloured pills spill over the floor:

or one arm hangs onto the swoop and lurch of a washbasin,
a rock-face with boot-marks scrabbling among ravines
    and clouds,

and that fantastically beautiful and silent fingerhold you never
    let go ...

Through bino's on a good day,
you can still see

the ghost of that red rope dangling from the sky.

On the Way to the Temple

A Kabuki doll stumbles up the street,
her stockings torn, mud
draggling her kimono,

blood in her hair, on her blue umbrella –

but it's only Cherry Spring in Toshogu,
with Almond blossom & white,
one shoe off & one shoe on.

Then a child points,
& everyone turns, everyone turns & looks.

But it's only a diamond tree by the river
stands in the last shower
with bare sun shining in its twigs,

it's only a Monk by the Vermilion Bridge
coughing quietly into a handkerchief.

His face rustles with leaves; waist-deep
    among the daffodils,
    his black glasses flashing

    Buddha! ... Buddha! ... Buddha!

Dit-da-dit

For fistulas and death – enter
the red mouth of the whale – a matchless

beached howl exploding gross blood and messages
in a Mars-coloured sea, electric grandeurs slippy with sperm
    and flame:

enter the slaughterhouse scream,
bearing the lethal waters of spilt images and madness.

It isn't easy being a giant
in a world of dwarfs;

dit-da-dit! dit-da-dit!

calling the dwarfs,
calling the dwarfs,
calling the dwarfs

Morse code/factory ship bottom of the world ...

where the sea-thundering ball-cock of the sun, ice-licked to
    lacquer, falls
like white-dust through the alchemy of stars

What's Japanese for –

'... O beautiful night-spirits of the deep /
    be your silence a divine globe of singing forever ...'

And how can we get there?

It's Money

Be it humble as this 1 Taka note – if it's money –
disregard whatever thumbmarks, patina of grime, grease,
Bangledeshi-chapati-paratha-hot-tomato-stains –

likewise those hundred million begging hands outstretched:

there are too many for you – too many hands of children in
   the dark,
those faces at night, those pale and sweet as ras malai,
as small round confections floating in thick milk.

In Madhupur, too many – those hands of the Mandi
   riceworkers,
the tree planters: and in Dhaka bazaars, in Chittagong
where the curved fingernails of beggars

wait all year for the night of *Shab-e-Barat*, the time
of giving which is Ramzan.

Or else, for too many, it's the wet, the monsoon turns:
   and there they go
in a blue torch of lightning – all the rubbish, the
   rikshas, mendicants,
ox-carts and cattle in the howling, everything away, away

into the Bay, all the people, all the children away,
limbs, hair by the Padma tossed, waters
of Jamuna streaming through open mouths,

dangled and tossed like puppets as the rain falls,
the rain falls,

the rain falls from
all the broken conch-shells of the moon.

And only money is immortal.

Boom!

Oh! he was!
Hemingway was beautiful!

When the mangy lion with agate eyes
and steel claws came out of the jungle –

Hemingway shot it.

When the buffalo with its filthy heart
would have gored him –

Hemingway shot it.

When the giraffe,
when the monkey,

Hemingway shot them.

Elephantszebraswilddogshogsleopardscheetahs vultures

and when they did –

       Booooommmmm!

But make no mistake, Hemingway
was beautiful: it was scary,

his eyes shone –

and in the famous opening paragraph
of his *Farewell to Arms* –

the leaves falling, the dust rising, the soldiers marching –

he wrote four sentences containing four commas and
   126 words —
of which one word contains three syllables,

twenty two have two,
103 have one ...

and, hiddden under the full stops, enough freakie-deakie
and asshole gun-poetry culture to blow up the world.

Back of Wordsworth

And don't you just love them back of the Langdales,
back of Wordsworth & Co. –

all those white jiddle sheep with their impeccable tongues
plunging their axes round a diddle wind ...

as they gambol through vermilion, piss, then snapdragon up
among the bracken with cloudlike hooves:

or squat there in the poem and shit black marbles: maybe three
  dozen in a pile ?

  (O dearest of Winander ! surprised by joy!)

But, it's got to be when Tom the Ostler vomits back of the fire
or the good wife passes by with a basket of dried screams on
  her arm –

and isn't this so splendidly by faith's transcendent dower?

Sweetest sheep!
I love those evening sonnets,

their silver springtime show
as they raise tails

and split moons – their little hooves plunging through daisies in a
  theme of silences.

Many's the time I've watched them in an 1800's sunset

with their gentle orifices squat-end into a widdle wind

while Dirk the bankrupt shepherd lifts his diddle smock
and pees onto a jiddle rock:

or coughs up a bloodied gob of T.B. phlegm by Grasmere's
    glassy lake

– some small rainbows by the cottages that still flutter
    on a bush
as a reminder.

Gallery

Let me walk you through

into that picture,
about six feet by six hanging on rough

white plaster in the Gallery:

non-English,
French, German, Etruscan?

But certainly wine –

that yellow, I can't get.
The yeellow of Pierro del Francesca,

the yeeelow of magicians.
The yeeelow in a sunrise creeping round the vichy-soisse of
   the world.

Or the yeeeeeelow of haystacks painted by Monet, dancing
   to bulls
and underlying all other colours in your mind.

Sweet Yeeeeeeeelow.

Pure Yeeeeeeeeeeeeeeelow on your tongue. Gesturing.
   Yewlo. Wllyoe.

That loud beating to Voodoodooddooddoo Yelowwwwyylloo.
To the dead faces of ylllllyewooo!

that yellowwwwwwwww,
falling behind me in the sunfalls of the picture

with the sound of bees through an open window.

If you compress lllllleyywwwwwooooollllyyyyyy far enough,
  long enough,
you fly by a misty lake at evening among black shadows

slanted over the polished floor of the Gallery,
with huge antennae and rainbow eyes,

sucking from the next huge white almond blossom pendulous
  on the walls.

Greensleeves

Love you *Greensleeves, baby* –

and you, impossibly fantastic screaming
white-shimmering
cinderish tarmac summer:

love you, beautiful lady of the icecream man's dreams,
his van melting, his heart melting

but still caroling *Greensleeves* through the loudspeaker

Alas my love you do me wrong

one tyre down, petrol exploding and backfiring –

but strumming his lyre OK

(up Elm St., down Oak)

*... for I have loved you O so long
and sigh for my Lady Greensleeves ...*

di da didi da dida da –

his hair marvellously on fire, the sky swallowing him all day,

– his small heroic Japanese Dalek and Chest Freezer

swivels from street to street

firing Mr. Whippy, Ice Cream Choc / Assorted
and Enormously Blue Flapping Tongues –

point-blank at the sun.

Pink

This is sweet as pink honey gets –

that crunchy rococo-sugar-heaven,
stucco on your eyelids,

bee-gunk on the roofs, dripping into flowers, roads,
chewinggum in your mouth . . .

like a nipple erect, a breast asleep that takes you
   by surprise . . .
suddenly shrieking Dufy! Dufy! La vie en rose –

as you rush out into the garden in a pair of soiled pyjamas
   to the Yes! Yes!
glow irridissimus and pure splendissimus of wallpaper

that's never been touched or sucked before: to watch, gaping,
that fantastic oofy-doofy sky-canvas, that nursery of
   smoking French

toilet seats wrapped in cyclamen and birthday paper,
   each cloud,
each moment of . . .

Love, Love and more Love.

In your nightwear dancing in it:
in your bottoms rolling in it –

dead bees from months before,
birdsong, caterpillars, scrolls and banknotes of more Egyptian
   weather forecasts,

. . . and to know, suddenly, everything on TV is true:

that nothing was ever meant – viz: your pink death, my
   pink death.

That, at any moment, a baby will appear from a red sky, smiling
   and kicking on the grass:

   Pol Pot, was never born

   The Jews were a conjuring trick

   And Hitler was a Magic Chocolate gobbled by Hysterectomies.

cartoons
&
characters

Maestro

Darth Vader in black,

clumped rolls of colour-coded wires,
the terrible sound of laboured breaths from an oxygen tank:

LCD flashes from his helmet and scrolls in Airport Arrivals

BEETHOVENBEETHOVENBEETHOVEN
CHOPINCHOPINCHOPINSTRAVINSKYSTRAVINSKY

barcarolles, mazurkas, symphonies . . .

violins, trumpets, drums, sheets of music floating through
    the air . . .

"Maestro – we welcome you to our humble city . . ."

his steps are ponderous,
a glint of metal behind the mask.

In the taxi on our way to the Opera House
2 small weeping dogs
in a cage . . .

his first meal.

Gift of the Magi

Strange light from Handel's star rolled on over that frozen snow:

Herod's bright sword feinted left and right;
giant oratorios leapt from his eyes,

his face crackled like gift-paper – for Rome, Caesar Augustus,
his fabulous fighters surrounded the Crib,

they zoomed round Palestine like wasps. Blood rags flapped in
   the wind.

And it was a dance of atoms, that slaughter of the innocents,
   a choreography
staged by flashing mirrors and the blind trumpets of Paradise …

as a door clanged open in hyper-space, haughtily, the Three Kings
stepped through a brilliant light of cross-fire lasers

into a Storm of Wormholes in the Strings of Time –

then vanished forever into the frozen vaults between the galaxies.

While Herod was left spinning like a top in the Forcefield of
   the Robots,
his finger pointing remorselessly towards Bethlehem.

Quiet Town

In squally rain, I'm staring out at the day, hoping for
    the best –
I am waiting for Virgil or Dante to show me the way:

I am looking for John Bunyan to conduct me to
    Le Café Warm
on the Rue des Miserables for a pie and cappuccino: my
    shoes leak,

water slops from my hat: an old man with a growth on
    his face hurries past,
a lone tram grinds through town – and there's a newsagent's.

On the next corner, near the Public Library and the
    Male Urinals –

I am considering my options

by a billboard obscured by mist – but featuring a
    red Ferrari
and a Malibu-blue sky ...

when this beautiful foxy Socialite in high heels and
    diamonds, holding
two lottery tickets, suddenly steps down from the poster
    and tosses me the keys.

She sticks a gun in my kisser and it's still raining.

> Now drive like hell! < she says.

Gumshoe

"It's my head on the block!" I said ...

and there was silence awhile.

I offered whiskey – but there were no takers.
Everyone was troubled: tough city cops – it gets them that way.

I swilled a toothmug and considered.

"There's no way ..." somebody began, then lapsed into silence.

"There's no way ..." continued maybe Arkady, Pel or
   the Commissioner,

"no one we can think of, no one in the Dept.,

no one in the city, in the world,
in the whole wide world:
we can think of nobody at all
in the world who might help you on that one ..."

There was silence awhile. So this was Goodbye Gents!
there would be no press statements.

In male bondings, there are No Regrets. No Tears.

When they got up to go, the floor shook,
the stairs shook.

From the window, I watched them going off
into the wild wet cold and mist

of the dark streets winding away around the world
where there was no one, absolutely no one,

no one they could think of
to help me at all ...

I watched them, twelve abreast, going down the street –

Japp, Pel, Gently, Menendez, Lemmy Caution, Taggart,
Arkady, Dalgliesh, Friday and Dupin, Maigret and Derek aus
    der Reihe.

As they all
climbed back into their story books and vanished.

                    *   *   *

Meanwhile, back in the Office,
it was my head on the block:

it sat there, blinking on the desk, beside the axe,
as blood leaked onto the floor.

While I prowled around it,
figuring my next move.

A Shorter
Chapman's Homer

The chaps were singing Hmhmm-Ohho-De-da-di-dee …

the chaps were off to The Wars,
no! they were sailing towards Ithaca, yes!
no! they were sailing away from Ithaca,

the chaps were pulling the oars.

Somewhere behind the winecasks, chaps Perimedes and Eurylochus
were being entertained by a little sailor chap

with starlight and ropeburns around his mouth.

It was the Time of Giants and Witchcraft: the day was fine,
   Ulysses was steering,
and round he went and round: he was off

to the Cannibal Isles again, he was Scissorman,
   he was Shakespeare
off to the Land of the Dead,

he was a one-man dance band, he was off his head –
and seventy violins were playing in his mouth.

   (but all the chaps kept singing Hoho-dee-di-dee-doh
   all the loyal and smelly chaps kept rowing him through
   the book.)

All the chaps were thinking about New York in the Sky.
All the chaps were thinking about running for President in
   Hindu Kush.

the wind blew:
the oxhide stays groaned

And most of the rest is lies.

Old Tarot

Somewhere, a needlestick dog howls —

and nearer to, waiting for the wrecker's ball, old midnight
    houses
lean together crazy as Tarot Cards in the rain:

lost souls peer through the dark — where, each night,
after the danse macabre and the ritual enactment of the
    hanged corpse,

a disemboweled head is placed under a lamppost in a pentacle
    of light.

Candles flicker: ghost shouts echo up stairwells —

while Madman, Junkie, Jester,
Old Mother Rotten on a Broom

wait for the night to happen.

When a car without lights, slowly kerb-cruises
through sweeping rain down the street at 1 a.m.

looking for a divine act of faith and ecstasy
with a twelve-year-old Madonna without the clap —

and the Green Dwarf slides down a Rope from the Sky —

you don't need a Crystal Ball.

Question

Is it with blood or not ...?

night in Castle Grimm/a thunderstorm,

as the old man with his enormously thick pebble-glasses peers
   into the toilet
and his wife joins him with her stick,

hunkering down

by the light of a torch, as they both stare
at a black turd floating in the pan.

And will it,
or won't it?

That is the question –

When the headless chair comes in ringing a handbell,
   it's 3 a.m. again:

*(through the windows, where lightning flickers over the town,
   another scene ...)*

lost souls, wind in the trees as brown clouds and black
seethe in contest like the forces of good and evil.

Then a Night Cart gallops past over the rim of the world,
   iron wheels –
tampons and brown-red-shit slopping behind –

vibrations of the dead; pillars gleam everywhere – those who
  looked back
and were struck to instant salt:

a cloak of stink from the sewage works,
we follow it to the end of time.

            *   *   *

Somewhere, a child: a stream of skulls in the storm:
but our feet slip on mucilage.

Deep under the hospital, we hear crying.
In a lift crowded with dead men, whisper of antennae as urine
  flakes at concrete,

cockroaches climb on the stopwatch of time.

Everywhich step we take,
wax ghosts with bad breath guard the way.

            *   *   *

First Voice –
in the doom of Castle Grimm,
night-emissions streaming down the window ...

Second Voice –
night terrors perceive encrypted demons at the heart of things;
computer generated clouds light with new voltages.

Third Voice –
from the black pit of prayers, the old man
kneels beside a pile of broken dreams.

He seeks the Master Blaster as the fear of entropy drifts through
   endless space. But only the Eye of The Jewelled One will do,
   a Diamond spinning at the centre of another dream –
   Amenamenamen.

*   *   *

But rectal pressures build –
small dark nucleii in cytoplasm drift through filthy labyrinths of
   encrusted dirt:

and then, weirdly, at the crossroads, by the Public Toilets –
a police car turned on its side, lights

redflash/redflash ...

Rain beats down
on an empty world:

an alien in a silver zoot, zipping him/herself/, emerges from
   the Gents.

Frowns and vanishes –

a pool of green water on the floor
crusted with curious isotopes –

Liposuction

Barf sucks
tallow-gah-gah-belch!

old yeller flubber-dubber –
of lipids and goose-blubby:

a plasm, 'gasm of plup, plub, plud!

with stale Yech! slippy on the door knobs of the Fat Clinic.

When pigfeed men collect goo ploop-vats –
you can hear buttock-flubber

blubber trying to climb out:

massive stone-age breasts with enormous eyelashes
leave grease-streaks and mascara all over the road.

A History of England

Chaucer, Lancaster, London:

when peasants danced the Morris – did –
so eldings flashed through MaGIC bELLS

and shone the sun down leafy lanes: but grim kinsmen
and the brilliance of the ring *were*

as The Finger moved:

only the throne *was*
from the beginning in the palace.

When Shakspere wrote his name, his only –
            Shaekspear,
            shaKSper

he scribbled in a margin –

and now helicopters whirl around his head forever.

In the depths of the Housing Estates,
only Merlin is left:

a dWArf, huGE -heADed,
who will lie here for a thousand years until England Needs
    Him again.

A STonE CrOsS iS buried in his SKull.

Ringwraiths

In 1050 of the Third Age of the Sun, an evil power came to the Forest of Greenwood the Great ... – Tolkien

Around the rotten tree they go –

their fungoid lips,
their swollen legs,

in the dRK OF NOWherE,
In ThE dRK MIRKWOOD.

(Around the rotten tree they go)

Around the rotten tree they go,
their sloppy bowels,
their staring eyes –

all blank from the hips down
as they all dance around the rotten tree.

All blank from the hips down,
like robots in the dark,

their huge yellow teeth,
black worm-goels writhing from their eyes,

as they all dance around the rotten tree
like robots in the dark.

But death still grabs them by the buttocks ...

Like Ringwraiths, with teeth and claws and huge sounds
    of flesh,

it hurls them down and around their heads at night.

And only children, screaming in their sleep,
soaked in sweat, snot on their lips when you pick them up,

wet and breath on your neck –

only children know,
curved back and screaming in your arms.

And there's no exorcism.

Envoi – Nature Diary

Laft night being
the firft night of the froft,

at the bottom of the garden,
I faw many wormx
curl and afleep:

then – where all the flowerx were dead –

by the path,
where the tender night-fpiritx lay ...

two ratx
gibbered and faffed at the moon.

All around lay fantafiex of doom
and ftarlit forboding whifpered by namelexx thingx.

In the dark of a hanging mirror,
I faw a man with one lip trying to fmile.

Wakefield Press has been publishing good Australian books
for over fifty years. For a catalogue of current and
forthcoming titles, or to add your name to our mailing list,
send your name and address to

Wakefield Press, Box 2266, Kent Town, South Australia 5071.

TELEPHONE (08) 8362 8800 FAX (08) 8362 7592
WEB www.wakefieldpress.com.au